SIMPLE MACHINES

PULLEY

Jeff Barger

Rourke
Educational Media

rourkeeducationalmedia.com

Before, During, and After Reading Activities

Before Reading: Building Background Knowledge and Academic Vocabulary

"Before Reading" strategies activate prior knowledge and set a purpose for reading. Before reading a book, it is important to tap into what your child or students already know about the topic. This will help them develop their vocabulary and increase their reading comprehension.

Questions and activities to build background knowledge:
1. *Look at the cover of the book. What will this book be about?*
2. *What do you already know about the topic?*
3. *Let's study the Table of Contents. What will you learn about in the book's chapters?*
4. *What would you like to learn about this topic? Do you think you might learn about it from this book? Why or why not?*

Building Academic Vocabulary
Building academic vocabulary is critical to understanding subject content.
Assist your child or students to gain meaning of the following vocabulary words.
Content Area Vocabulary
Read the list. What do these words mean?

- *advantage*
- *complex*
- *effort*
- *force*
- *inclined*
- *load*

During Reading: Writing Component

"During Reading" strategies help to make connections, monitor understanding, generate questions, and stay focused.
1. *While reading, write in your reading journal any questions you have or anything you do not understand.*
2. *After completing each chapter, write a summary of the chapter in your reading journal.*
3. *While reading, make connections with the text and write them in your reading journal.*
   a) Text to Self – What does this remind me of in my life? What were my feelings when I read this?
   b) Text to Text – What does this remind me of in another book I've read? How is this different from other books I've read?
   c) Text to World – What does this remind me of in the real world? Have I heard about this before? (News, current events, school, etc....)

After Reading: Comprehension and Extension Activity

"After Reading" strategies provide an opportunity to summarize, question, reflect, discuss, and respond to text. After reading the book, work on the following questions with your child or students to check their level of reading comprehension and content mastery.
1. *How do pulleys make work easier? (Summarize)*
2. *Why do we need pulleys? (Infer)*
3. *What are two pulleys that you would find in a home or at a school? (Asking Questions)*
4. *Name a pulley that you have seen or used in the last week. (Text to Self Connection)*

Extension Activity
Look at the ceiling of your classroom. Think of two or more items that would need to be lifted above the ceiling to be used. Brainstorm how those items would be lifted that high.

TABLE OF CONTENTS

The Super Six

Think about your breakfast. Did you drink milk today? If it came from a jug, you used a machine. Did you spread butter on toast? You used a machine. The cap on the milk is a screw. A butter knife is a wedge. Screws and wedges are simple machines.

Use of simple machines started long ago. They make work easier. You use less **effort**. The claw of a hammer is a simple machine. You use this lever to pull a nail. This beats using your hand.

Examples of simple machines date back several thousand years.

There are six types of simple machines. Each one has few parts. One kind is an **inclined** plane. A ramp is an inclined plane. It lifts loads like boxes or cars. A slide is another inclined plane.

inclined plane

The six simple machines are the wheel and axle, inclined plane, lever, pulley, screw, wedge, and wheel.

wheel and axle

The wheel and axle is a simple machine. Carrying heavy bags is hard. Using a cart is easy. Wheels on the cart allow us to use less effort.

What Is a Pulley?

Flagpoles use a simple machine. It is called a pulley. A grooved, or cut, wheel holds a cable or rope. The flag is connected to the rope.

The wheel in a pulley is also known as a drum.

pulley

Pulling on the rope lifts the flag. Thanks to the groove, the rope stays in place. An axle turns the wheel. Pulleys can reach areas of great height.

Pulleys can be found in many places. Curtains open and close. Water comes from a well. Blinds close in your house. Elevators go up and down. All of these use pulleys.

There are three types of pulleys. All of them are built to carry a **load**. Each one uses a rope or cable too. How they carry the load is the difference.

The three types of pulleys are fixed, movable, and compound.

A fixed pulley is being used in this rescue. The pulley moves with the cable.

Fixed Pulleys

The wheel in a fixed pulley does not move. Fixed means staying in one place. Go back to the flagpole. At the top, a wheel is connected to the pole.

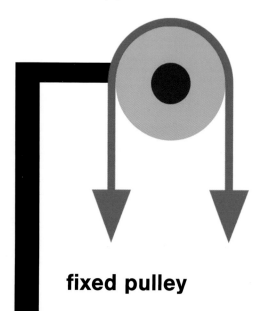

fixed pulley

A dumbwaiter is a pulley that is a mini-elevator. It is used to move objects within a building.

Pull on the rope. The flag, or load, will move up. You are changing the direction of the **force**. Blinds on a window work the same way. Pull the cord and the blinds go up or down.

A fishing rod is a **complex** machine, which is made up of two or more simple machines. The rod is a lever.

You use a fixed pulley to go fishing. The reel on a fishing rod is a pulley. Winding the line is like raising a flag. The load is on the end. If you're lucky, that load will be a big fish!

Maybe sailing is more your speed. A sailboat uses a fixed pulley. It lifts the sail. The sail moves on a pole. The pole is called a mast.

Movable Pulleys

A movable pulley is not fixed. It can move up or down. It moves with the load. A movable pulley can lower a flower basket for watering.

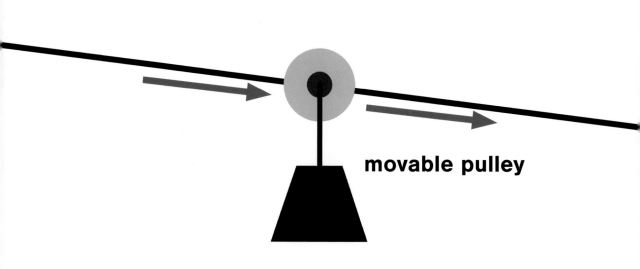

movable pulley

Zip lines use a movable pulley. They travel from a higher spot to a lower one. The line is a rope or cable. Moving along the line is the pulley. The person is the load.

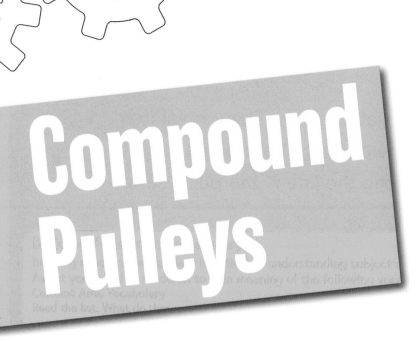

Compound Pulleys

A blend of fixed and movable pulleys is a compound pulley. It is also called a block and tackle. The pulleys are the blocks. They work together. This allows more weight to be lifted.

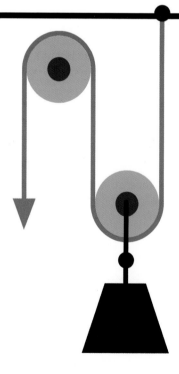

compound pulley

Mechanical advantage is what you gain by using a machine instead of just your own force.

Cranes use this for extra mechanical advantage. The movable pulley is closest to the load. Further away is the fixed pulley.

Look up at a skyscraper. Is somebody washing windows? They are using a pulley to move up and down. Rock climbers use pulleys too. Lifting heavy loads is difficult work. Why not get some help? Pulleys make work easier. Saving effort is a smart move.

Activity: Build a Pulley

Building a pulley is easy. Here's an activity to show you how.

Supplies

- doorknob
- roll of string/thread/yarn
- recycled plastic fruit cup
- single hole punch
- paper clip
- tape measure
- scissors

Directions

1. Find a door in your classroom or house. The doorknob will be the axle for the pulley.

2. Use a tape measure to measure a piece of string eight inches (20.32 centimeters). Cut the string.

3. Punch a single hole on both sides of the recycled fruit cup.

4. Place the string through the holes and tie a knot above the fruit cup.

5. Measure the distance from the doorknob to the floor. Use this length to cut a second piece of string.

6. Tie the second piece of string to the first piece above the fruit cup.

7. Place a small number of paper clips in the fruit cup.

8. Run the long piece of string around the doorknob and pull the string.

Now you have a pulley!

GLOSSARY

advantage (uhd-VAN-tij): something that helps you or puts you ahead

complex (KAHM-pleks): having a large number of parts

effort (EF-urt): the activity of trying hard to achieve something

force (fors): any action that produces, stops, or changes the shape or the movement of an object

inclined (in-KLINDE): leaning or slanting

load (lohd): something heavy or bulky that is being carried or is about to be carried

Load

Effort

Using a pulley makes light work of lifting a heavy load! The effort force is smaller than the load force.

INDEX

SHOW WHAT YOU KNOW

1. Name an object that is a wedge.

2. What is the work done by a pulley?

3. Why might someone salute a pulley?

4. Name two objects that use pulleys and move people.

5. How can a pulley make a tall building cleaner?

FURTHER READING

Adler, David A., *Simple Machines: Wheels, Levers, and Pulleys*, Holiday House, 2015.

Manley, Erika S., *Pulleys*, Jump! Inc., 2018.

Rustad, Martha E.H., *Pulleys*, Capstone Press, 2018.

ABOUT THE AUTHOR

Jeff Barger is an author, blogger, and literacy specialist. He lives in North Carolina. He once used a pulley to catch a fish that got away.

Meet The Author!
www.meetREMauthors.com

www.rourkeeducationalmedia.com

PHOTO CREDITS: Cover and Title ©mrfotos; Pg 3, 5, 6, 9, 10, 12, 15, 16, ©lolon; Pg 5, 6, 8, 11, 12, 14, 19, ©eriksvoboda; Pg 1, 3, 5, 6, 7, 8, 9, 10, 11, 12, 13, 14, 15, 16, 17, 18, 19, 20, 21, 22, 23, 24 ©Amtitus; Pg 4 ©Spauln, ©Michael Burrell; Pg 5 ©Eerik, Pg 6 ©Photitos2016; Pg 7 ©Image Source; Pg 8 ©RoschetzkyIstockPhoto; Pg 9 ©Anetlanda; Pg 10 ©pattonmania, ©empire331; Pg 11 ©fabphoto; Pg 12 ©WIKI, ©Bibica; Pg 13 ©By Robert Heber; Pg 14 ©Robert Daly; Pg 15 ©zoranm; Pg 16 ©WIKI, ©joyt; Pg 17 ©JHVEPhoto; Pg 18 ©WIKI; Pg 19 ©HHakim; Pg 20 ©beyhan yazar; Pg 21 ©rambo182, ©nongnewnun12; Pg 22 ©vau902

Edited by: Keli Sipperley
Cover and interior design by: Rhea Magaro-Wallace

Library of Congress PCN Data

Pulley / Jeff Barger
(Simple Machines)
ISBN 978-1-64369-041-4 (hard cover)
ISBN 978-1-64369-097-1 (soft cover)
ISBN 978-1-64369-188-6 (e-Book)
Library of Congress Control Number: 2018955960

Rourke Educational Media
Printed in the United States of America,
North Mankato, Minnesota